What You Don't Know about Retirement....

A Funny Retirement Quiz

Bill Dodds

Meadowbrook Press
Distributed by Simon & Schuster
New York

Library of Congress Cataloging-in-Publication Data

Dodds, Bill.

What you don't know about retirement: a funny retirement quiz / Bill Dodds.

p. cm.

ISBN 0-88166-359-X (Meadowbrook)—ISBN 0-671-31817-9 (Simon & Schuster)

1. Retirement—Humor. I. Title.

PN6231.R44 D63 2000

—dc21   99-058494

Managing Editor: Christine Zuchora-Walske

Coordinating Editor: Joseph Gredler

Production Manager: Paul Woods

Desktop Publishing: Danielle White

Illustrator: Steve Mark

© 2000 by Bill Dodds

Published by Meadowbrook Press, 5451 Smetana Drive, Minnetonka, MN 55343

www.meadowbrookpress.com

BOOK TRADE DISTRIBUTION by Simon & Schuster, a division of Simon and Schuster, Inc., 1230 Avenue of the Americas, New York, NY 10020

03 02 01 00   10 9 8 7 6 5 4 3 2 1

Printed in the United States of America

Contents

Dedication

In loving memory of my father, John J. Dodds,
a federal employee for thirty years
and a retiree for twenty-five.

A Day in the Life

Chapter 1

Q: What do retirees find hardest about their new status?

A: *Paying for photocopies.*

Q: What most amazes new retirees?

A: They're so busy now, they don't know how they ever had time for work.

Q: What's the primary cause of new retirees' disorientation and confusion?

A: *Lack of stress.*

Q: Why don't retirees protest the stereotype that says they're either hyperactive or always napping?

A: They're either too busy to care what other people say, or they're asleep.

Q: What's the retiree's favorite bumper sticker?

A: *"Go ahead and pass. What do I care?"*

Q: How do retirees measure time?

A: By how often the batteries in the TV remote have to be replaced.

Q: Just how much free time does a retiree have?

A: *Enough to actually stay on the line until her call to the HMO, government agency, or computer help line is answered by a human being.*

Q: What do retirees like to eat for breakfast?

A: *Lunch.*

Q: What do retirees call a long lunch?

A: *Normal.*

Q: What are retirees experts at?

A: Telling the difference between late breakfast, brunch, and early lunch.

Q: What does a retiree consider a well-balanced meal?

A: One that doesn't tip off his lap as he watches Wheel of Fortune.

Q: How does a retiree explain the difference between "napping," "dozing," and "resting my eyes" in the living room?

A: If she's all alone, she's "napping." If someone calls, she's "dozing." If someone enters the room and sees her, she's only "resting her eyes."

14

Q: How do retired executives spend most afternoons?

A: *Power napping.*

Q: When is a retiree's bedtime?

A: *Three hours after he falls asleep on the sofa watching TV.*

Q: Why don't retirees mind being called "senior citizens"?

A: The term comes with a 10 percent discount.

18

Q: What are the greatest perks of retirement?

A: *Running errands in the middle of the day and never standing in line.*

Q: I'm thinking about moving into a retirement community. What's the biggest disadvantage?

A: *If you're under seventy, and another resident needs anything moved or lifted, he or she will "ask the youngster."*

Q: What's the difference between a worker starting retirement and a young student starting summer vacation?

A: Summer ends.

Q: Why do retirees hate holidays?

A: There are too many workers with the day off cluttering up stores and movie theaters.

Q: Why does a recent retiree feel as if he's walking on air?

A: *He's got a monkey off his back and a load off his mind.*

24

The New Work Ethic

Chapter 2

Q: What's the best way to describe retirement?

A: *The coffee break that never ends.*

Q: What does a retiree consider a productive morning?

A: *Finding all six different items in the newspaper's Jumble puzzle.*

28

Q: What's the difference between a birdhouse built by a Cub Scout and a birdhouse built by a retiree?

A: Three weeks, seventeen trips to the hardware store, and about $1,500 worth of power tools.

Q: What is the retirees' "work ethic"?

A: Any job worth doing is worth dragging out.

Q: How do retirees reply when asked, "What do you do all day?"

A: *"I've never been so busy in my life."*

Q: What's the perfect second career for most retirees?

A: *Couch tester.*

Q: What's the most frequent excuse retirees use when abandoning a task around the house?

A: *"I want to save something to do tomorrow."*

Q: How does a retiree make sure all the items on her daily to-do list are checked off?

A: *She doesn't write any jobs on it until they're already done.*

Q: What's the Retirees' Motto?

A: "Thank God It's Monday."

Q: What's the difference between daylight-saving time and "retiree's time"?

A: Daylight-saving time is an hour ahead of standard time. Retiree's time is "when I'm darned good and ready, that's when."

Q: How many retirees does it take to change a light bulb?

A: *Only one, but it might take all day.*

Q: What's the biggest complaint among retirees?

A: *There's not enough time to get everything done.*

Fashion

Chapter 3

Q: Why is it wrong to stereotype retirees as spending most mornings lounging around in their robes and slippers?

A: *Some don't wear slippers.*

42

Q: What's the difference between casual office wear and a retiree's favorite outfit?

A: *Casual office wear doesn't include pajamas.*

44

Q: How does a retiree know it's time for lunch?

A: He starts to feel guilty about still being in his pajamas.

Q: Why do most retirees enjoy bonfires?

A: Discarded neckties or pantyhose burns well.

Q: Among retirees, what's considered formal attire?

A: *Tied shoes.*

48

Family

Chapter 4

Q: What are the greatest concerns for two retirees considering getting married?

A: *Will my family accept my new spouse? And is this going to mess up my Social Security benefits?*

Q: What's a good location for a new retiree with adult children?

A: *Close enough to see them as often as you like; far enough away that they can't just pop in unannounced.*

Q: What do you call a grandparent who's taken care of the little ones on Saturday and Sunday?

A: Re-tired.

Q: Why are retirees so slow to clean out the basement, attic, or garage?

A: They know as soon as they do, one of their adult kids will ask to store stuff there.

Q: How can I make sure my friends and family stay in touch?

A: *Move to a vacation spot and live in a place with a pool.*

54

Q: When does a retiree finally feel old?

A: *When one of her kids retires.*

Money

Chapter 5

Q: Why do so many retirement books focus on income?

A: During their working years, retirees got used to eating.

58

Q: Why do retirees' expenses drop so suddenly after they quit working?

A: *No more antacids.*

Q: What's always the first advice offered by any retirement planner?

A: "You should have started saving twenty years ago."

Q: What are a retiree's two greatest fears?

A: (1) The money will run out before his life ends. (2) His life will end before the money runs out.

61

Q: How do retirees refer to the Social Security payments deducted from young workers' paychecks?

A: *My friend FICA.*

Q: What's most startling about a retiree's first pension check?

A: It's so much bigger than her first paycheck and buys so much less.

Q: Why do retirees count pennies?

A: They're the only ones who have the time.

Q: What's the difference between a retiree who's frugal and one who's cheap?

A: *You're frugal; he's cheap.*

Q: My friends seem jealous because I've made a lot of money in my high-tech job and I'm retiring even though I'm only in my thirties. What should I do?

A: *Go to hell.*

Q: What do you call someone rich enough to retire very young?

A: *Mr. Gates.*

Q: What's the difference between a consultant and an employee?

A: A consultant makes 25 percent more and doesn't have an ulcer.

Q: What are the advantages and disadvantages of selling my house?

A: The advantage is some young couple will offer you more money than you made in your entire life. The disadvantage is you'll have to pack.

Recreation

Chapter 6

Q: What's the advantage of going back to school as a retiree?

A: If you cut classes, no one calls your parents.

Q: I've been thinking about traveling after I retire. Any suggestions?

A: *Many new retirees enjoy driving by the old workplace in the middle of the workday.*

Q: How has the Internet changed retirement?

A: *Now retirees can keep up on stupid office jokes via e-mail.*

74

Q: What's the best way for a retiree to make sure her memoirs are read?

A: Include lots of clues about hidden money.

Q: Why do retirees make such good babysitters?

A: Decades of dealing with bosses have made them experts at handling two-year-olds.

Q: Why is it dangerous for a retiree to miss his condo-owners association meeting?

A: He might be elected president.

Q: What's the nickname for retirees who don't travel south each winter?

A: Penguins.

Q: What's the only difference between recently married retirees and teen-age newlyweds?

A: *Fifty years.*

Q: What do you call a retiree on vacation?

A: Redundant.

Q: Why don't retired nurses like to give toasts?

A: They're tired of saying "bottoms up."

Health and Medicine

Chapter 7

Q: What's the most important key to a successful retirement?

A: *Don't die on the job.*

Q: What do you call a retired professional ballplayer?

A: A thirty-year-old multimillionaire with bad knees.

Q: I have a friend who recently retired. Now, for no apparent reason, he suddenly bursts out laughing. Is he crazy?

A: *No. He's happy.*

Q: I've noticed many new retirees suddenly take a great interest in improving their health. Why is this?

A: *Now they have a reason to live.*

Q: What's the easiest way to deal with the Medicare system?

A: *Never get sick.*

Q: How long can the average retiree expect to live after retirement?

A: *Not long enough.*

Q: Why do new retirees suddenly look ten years younger?

A: They suddenly feel ten years younger.

Q: What's the most common observation among retirees?

A: *"People my age aren't as old as they used to be."*

Calling It Quits

Chapter 8

Q: What's the common term for someone who enjoys her work so much, she refuses to retire?

A: *Nuts.*

Q: Coworkers keep asking me what I'm going to do after I retire. I'm not sure. What should I say?

A: *"Not this."*

Q: Why do so many people have to wait until they're in their sixties or seventies before retiring?

A: *They're not good at picking lottery numbers.*

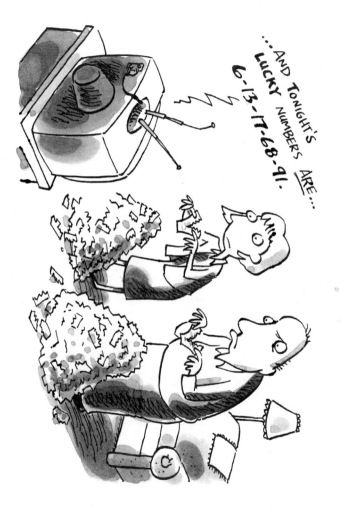

Q: How do I know if I'm old enough to join the American Association of Retired Persons?

A: You are if you notice they accept fifty-year-olds and you think, "Gee, that young?"

Q: Wouldn't it be better for people to retire when they're younger?

A: No! It's bad enough youth is wasted on the young. Retirement shouldn't be, too.

Q: What's the biggest advantage of retiring at age sixty-two?

A: *Not working at age sixty-three.*

Q: How do you know when it's time for you to retire?

A: Your supervisor is the granddaughter of your first boss, you remember what the company did for the Bicentennial, and you're the only one who knows how to "work" carbon paper.

101

Q: Will my relationship with my boss change after I announce I'm going to retire?

A: Yes. It will improve dramatically because it's much easier to get along with a supervisor when you realize you don't care what he or she thinks, says, or does.

Q: Should I still go to staff meetings after I've announced my retirement?

A: *You may want to attend, since you can now say whatever comes to mind.*

103

Q: I've heard that upper management is often given a "Golden Elevator"—a big promotion—just before retiring. What can the rest of us expect?

A: *The Royal Shaft.*

Q: What do you call a retired boss?

A: Anything you want.

105

Q: What's the key to really enjoying an office retirement party?

A: *Being the guest of honor.*

Q: What are the keys to a good farewell speech?

A: Be kind, be brief, be gone.

107

Q: Why is it no longer common to give a retiree a watch?

A: *It finally dawned on personnel departments that retired folks don't care what time it is.*

Q: What's a better retirement gift than a gold watch?

A: Being allowed to keep your expense account.

Q: I've noticed a lot of my coworkers are stopping by to say good-bye and wish me well. Aren't they nice?

A: Not really. They're checking out what furniture, equipment, and supplies they can "acquire" the moment you step out the door.

Q: What's the advantage of staying on the job beyond retirement age?

A: *At any time, for any reason, you can tell a boss, customer, or fellow employee to "drop dead" and walk out the door.*

Q: What's the difference between the last dragged-out six months of high school and the last dragged-out six months of work?

A: *Prom.*

Q: How is the first day on the job like the last day there?

A: *You think it will never end.*

Q: How is the last day on the job a lot like dying?

A: Heaven comes next.

115

Q: Who invented retirement?

A: *God, who worked for six days* and then retired.

Missing the Old Job

Chapter 9

Q: Why does a retiree often say he doesn't miss the job but he misses the people he used to work with?

A: *He's too polite to tell the whole truth.*

Q: How is retiring different from going on an annual vacation?

A: A retiree doesn't have to put in overtime to get all her work done before she leaves.

Q: What's the best indication a retiree has done his job well?

A: It's taken two people and a computer program to replace him.

Q: What makes a retiree's heart soar?

A: Hearing the company has gone downhill since she left, but the pension plan is safe.

Q: I hate to admit it, but some days I miss work. What can I do?

A: Listen to rush-hour traffic reports.

Order Form

Qty.	Title	Author	Order #	Unit Cost (U.S. $)	Total
	Age Happens	Lansky, B.	4025	$7.00	
	Are You over the Hill?	Dodds, B.	4265	$7.00	
	How to Survive Your 40th Birthday	Dodds, B.	4260	$7.00	
	What's So Funny About Getting Old?	Fischer/Noland	4205	$7.00	
	What You Don't Know about Turning 50	Witte, P.D.	4085	$6.00	
	You're No Spring Chicken	Fischer, E.	4215	$7.00	
				Subtotal	
			Shipping and Handling (see below)		
			MN residents add 6.5% sales tax		
				Total	

YES! Please send me the books indicated above. Add $2.00 shipping and handling for the first book with a retail price up to $9.99, or $3.00 for the first book with a retail price over $9.99. Add $1.00 shipping and handling for each additional book. All orders must be prepaid. Most orders are shipped within two days by U.S. Mail (7–9 delivery days). Rush shipping is available for an extra charge. Overseas postage will be billed. **Quantity discounts available upon request.**

Send book(s) to:

Name _____

Address _____

City _____ State _____ Zip _____ Telephone (____) _____

Payment via: ☐ Check or money order payable to Meadowbrook Press

☐ Visa (for orders over $10.00 only)   ☐ MasterCard (for orders over $10.00 only)

Account # _____ Signature _____ Exp. Date _____

A FREE Meadowbrook Press catalog is available upon request.

Mail to: Meadowbrook Press, 5451 Smetana Drive, Minnetonka, MN 55343

Phone: 612-930-1100   Toll-Free: 800-338-2232   Fax: 612-930-1940

For more information (and fun) visit our website: www.meadowbrookpress.com